Mediter~ Cookb~

Mediterranean-~ ~cipes for Preconception, Pregn ~cy & Egg Fertility

By

Rachel Carter

Copyright © 2024 by Rachel Carter

Table of Contents

INTRODUCTION

Jennifer Lawson had always dreamed of becoming a mother. But after years of trying, she was diagnosed with infertility and told that her chances of conceiving naturally were very low. She felt hopeless and depressed until she discovered the IVF Mediterranean recipes. The IVF Mediterranean recipes were a collection of dishes that were designed to boost fertility, balance hormones, and prepare the body for pregnancy. They were based on the principles of the Mediterranean diet, which emphasized fresh fruits, vegetables, whole grains, fish, olive oil, and nuts. Jennifer decided to give it a try and followed the recipes religiously for three months.

She was amazed by the results. Not only did she feel healthier and happier, but she also noticed a positive change in her ovulation and menstrual cycles. She decided to undergo an IVF treatment and hoped for the best. To her delight, the treatment was successful and she became pregnant with her first child. Jennifer was overjoyed and grateful. She continued to follow the IVF Mediterranean recipes throughout her pregnancy and gave birth to a healthy baby girl. She named her Sophia, which means wisdom in Greek. She felt that her daughter was a gift from the gods and a testament to the power of the IVF Mediterranean recipes.

CHAPTER ONE

Understanding the Mediterranean Diet for IVF

Understanding the Mediterranean Diet for In Vitro Fertilization (IVF) involves delving into a dietary pattern renowned for its emphasis on whole, nutrient-dense foods inspired by the traditional eating habits of Mediterranean regions. At its core, the Mediterranean Diet for IVF emphasizes fresh fruits and vegetables, whole grains, lean proteins, and healthy fats, with olive oil often taking a central role. This dietary approach encourages a moderate intake of fish and poultry while limiting red meat and processed foods. The incorporation of legumes, nuts, and seeds adds plant-based protein sources, contributing to a well-rounded nutritional profile. Furthermore, the Mediterranean Diet for IVF values the consumption of foods rich in antioxidants, vitamins, and minerals, which are integral for supporting overall health. The inclusion of omega-3 fatty acids, prevalent in fish and olive oil, aligns with its cardiovascular benefits. By fostering a balanced intake of macronutrients and prioritizing fresh, seasonal ingredients, this diet seeks to create a foundation that complements the complexities of fertility treatments. For those undergoing IVF, knowing the subtleties of this nutritional strategy is crucial since it offers a foundation for making educated food decisions that support their objectives for reproductive health.

Why Choose the Mediterranean Diet for IVF?

Choosing the Mediterranean Diet for In Vitro Fertilization (IVF) is rooted in the holistic and nutrient-rich nature of this eating pattern. The Mediterranean Diet stands out for its emphasis on whole, unprocessed foods that offer a diverse array of essential nutrients. This diet prioritizes fresh fruits, vegetables, whole grains, lean proteins, and healthy fats, such as those found in olive oil and fatty fish. The incorporation of plant-based proteins, like legumes and nuts, further enriches the nutritional profile, providing a spectrum of vitamins and minerals crucial for reproductive health.

The Mediterranean Diet's focus on antioxidants, omega-3 fatty acids, and anti-inflammatory properties aligns with the intention to create an optimal environment for fertility treatments. It promotes cardiovascular health, supports hormonal balance, and may positively impact reproductive outcomes. Additionally, its sustainable and enjoyable nature makes it a viable long-term lifestyle choice. Choosing the Mediterranean Diet for IVF is a proactive step towards fostering overall well-being, offering a balanced foundation that complements the intricate journey of assisted reproductive technologies. This dietary approach is not just about sustenance but embraces the broader concept of nourishing the body to enhance the chances of success in the IVF process.

Foods to Eat and Avoid

The In Vitro Fertilization (IVF) Mediterranean diet emphasizes nutrient-dense foods that can potentially support reproductive health.

Foods to Eat:

Vegetables and Fruits: The foundation of any diet, they are abundant in vitamins, minerals, and antioxidants. Berries, leafy greens, and colorful vegetables contribute to a diverse nutrient profile.

Whole Grains: Opt for whole grains like quinoa, brown rice, and whole wheat, providing complex carbohydrates for sustained energy.

Lean Proteins: Include Foods such as fish, poultry, legumes, and tofu. These offer essential amino acids and support muscle health.

Healthy Fats: Olive oil, avocados, and nuts contain monounsaturated fats and omega-3 fatty acids, contributing to cardiovascular health and hormonal balance.

Dairy or Alternatives: Include dairy or fortified alternatives for calcium and vitamin D, crucial for bone health.

Foods to Avoid or Limit:

Processed Foods: Minimize the intake of processed and refined foods, which may contain additives and preservatives.

Red and Processed Meat: Limit red and processed meats, opting for leaner protein sources to reduce saturated fat intake.

Added Sugars: Reduce consumption of sugary snacks and beverages to manage blood sugar levels.

Highly Caffeinated Drinks: Limit caffeine intake as excessive amounts may impact fertility. Opt for herbal teas or decaffeinated options.

Excessive Alcohol: Moderation is key; excessive alcohol can affect hormonal balance.

Balancing the Mediterranean diet for IVF involves prioritizing whole, nutrient-rich foods while minimizing processed and potentially inflammatory choices. Personalization based on individual health considerations and preferences is essential for optimizing the benefits of this dietary approach during the IVF journey.

Getting Started with the Mediterranean Diet for IVF

Getting started with the Mediterranean Diet for In Vitro Fertilization (IVF) involves gradual and sustainable changes to dietary habits. Begin by incorporating abundant fruits, vegetables, and whole grains into daily meals. Prioritize lean proteins such as fish, legumes, and poultry, along with healthy fats from olive oil and nuts. Replace refined grains with whole grains for increased fiber and nutrient content. Experiment with Mediterranean herbs and spices to enhance flavor without relying on excessive salt. Stay hydrated with water and herbal teas. Gradually reduce processed foods, red meat, and sugary snacks. Consult with your healthcare provider or nutritionist for personalized guidance, ensuring the diet aligns with specific health needs and complements the IVF process effectively. Embracing the Mediterranean Diet is not just a nutritional shift but a holistic lifestyle approach to support reproductive health during IVF.

Essential Nutrients for Reproductive Health

Essential nutrients play a fundamental role in maintaining reproductive health for both men and women. These nutrients contribute to hormonal balance, support fertility, and ensure a healthy environment for conception.

For Women

Folate: Essential for preventing neural tube defects in early pregnancy, found in leafy greens and fortified foods.

Iron: Critical for preventing anemia and supporting blood flow to reproductive organs, sourced from lean meats, beans, and spinach.

Calcium: Vital for bone health and muscle function, sourced from dairy or fortified plant-based alternatives.

For Men

Zinc: Crucial for sperm production and motility, present in oysters, nuts, and seeds.

Vitamin C: Supports sperm quality and protects against oxidative stress, found in citrus fruits and berries.

Omega-3 Fatty Acids: Linked to improved sperm morphology, sourced from fatty fish, flaxseeds, and walnuts.

General Nutrients

Vitamin D: Essential for hormonal balance, obtained from sunlight, fatty fish, and fortified foods.

Antioxidants: Found in fruits, vegetables, and nuts, they protect reproductive cells from oxidative damage.

Protein: Crucial for tissue repair and hormone production, sourced from lean meats, dairy, legumes, and plant-based proteins.

A balanced diet rich in these essential nutrients, along with a healthy lifestyle, contributes to optimal reproductive health, fostering the conditions necessary for a successful conception and a healthy pregnancy.

CHAPTER TWO

Breakfast Recipes

Greek Yogurt Bowl with Berries and Nuts

Serving: One

Ingredients:
- 1 cup Greek yogurt
- 1/2 cup mixed berries
- 1/4 cup chopped nuts (almonds, walnuts, or pistachios)
- 1 tsp honey

Preparation:

1. Place the Greek yogurt in a bowl.

2. Top with mixed berries and chopped nuts.

3. Drizzle with honey.

Approximate Nutritional Value:
Calories: 300
Protein: 20g
Fat: 15g
Carbohydrates: 20g
Fiber: 5g

Mediterranean Flatbread Pizza

Serving: One

Ingredients:
- 1 whole-grain flatbread
- 1/4 cup tomato sauce
- 1/4 cup chopped spinach
- 1/4 cup chopped red bell pepper
- 1/4 cup crumbled feta cheese
- 1 tsp olive oil
- Salt and pepper

Preparation:

1. Preheat the oven to 400°F.

2. Spread the tomato sauce on the flatbread.

3. Add the spinach, red bell pepper, and feta cheese.

4. Drizzle with olive oil and sprinkle with salt and pepper.

5. Bake for 10-12 minutes or until the cheese is melted and bubbly.

Approximate Nutritional Value:

Calories: 400

Protein: 20g

Fat: 20g

Carbohydrates: 40g

Fiber: 10g

Turkish Menemen

Serving: One

Ingredients:
- 2 eggs
- 2 tomatoes
- 1/2 green pepper
- 1/2 onion
- 2 tbsp olive oil
- Salt and pepper

Preparation:
1. Heat the olive oil in a pan.

2. Add the chopped onion and green pepper, and sauté until soft.

3. Add the chopped tomatoes and cook until they soften.

4. Crack the eggs over the tomato mixture.

5. Cook until the eggs are done to your liking.

6. Season with salt and pepper

Approximate Nutritional Value:
Calories: 200
Protein: 10g
Fat: 10g
Carbohydrates: 10g
Fiber: 3g

Avocado and Tomato Toast

Serving: One

Ingredients:
- 1 slice of whole-grain bread
- 1/2 ripe avocado
- 1/2 tomato
- 1 egg
- 1 tsp olive oil

•Salt and pepper

Preparation:

1. Toast the bread.

2. Mash the avocado and spread it on the toast.

3. Slice the tomato and place it on top of the avocado.

4. Fry the egg in olive oil and place it on top of the tomato.

5. Sprinkle with salt and pepper

Approximate Nutritional Value:
Calories: 400
Protein: 20g
Fat: 30g
Carbohydrates: 20g   Fiber: 10g

Mediterranean Veggie Omelette

Serving: One

Ingredients:
- 2 eggs
- 1/4 cup chopped spinach
- 1/4 cup chopped red bell pepper
- 1/4 cup chopped onion
- 1/4 cup crumbled feta cheese
- 1 tsp olive oil
- Salt and pepper

Preparation:

1. Beat the eggs in a bowl and add salt and pepper.

2. Heat the olive oil in a non-stick pan.

3. Add the spinach, red bell pepper, and onion and sauté for 2-3 minutes.

4. Pour the eggs over the vegetables and cook until set.

5. Sprinkle the feta cheese on top and fold the omelet in half.

Approximate Nutritional Value:
Calories: 300
Protein: 20g
Fat: 20g
Carbohydrates: 10g
Fiber: 3g

Mediterranean Shakshuka

Serving: One

Ingredients:
•2 eggs
•1/2 onion
•1/2 red bell pepper
•1 garlic clove

- 1/2 tsp cumin
- 1/2 tsp paprika
- 1/4 tsp cayenne pepper
- 1 can diced tomatoes
- 1 tbsp olive oil
- Salt and pepper

Preparation:

1. Heat the olive oil in a pan.

2. Add the chopped onion and red bell pepper, and sauté until soft.

3. Add the minced garlic, cumin, paprika, and cayenne pepper, and cook for 1-2 minutes.

4. Add the diced tomatoes and simmer for 5-10 minutes.

5. Crack the eggs over the tomato mixture.

6. Cover the pan and cook until the eggs are done to your liking. Season with salt and pepper.

Approximate Nutritional Value:
Calories: 300
Protein: 10g
Fat: 20g
Carbohydrates: 20g
Fiber: 5g

Smoked Salmon and Cream Cheese Bagel

Serving: One

Ingredients:
• 1 whole-grain bagel
• 2 oz smoked salmon
• 2 tbsp cream cheese
• 1/4 red onion (thinly sliced)
• 1 tbsp capers

Preparation:

1. Toast the bagel.

2. Spread the cream cheese on the bagel.

3. Top with smoked salmon, red onion, and capers.

Approximate Nutritional Value:
Calories: 400
Protein: 20g
Fat: 20g
Carbohydrates: 30g
Fiber: 5g

Frittata with Vegetables and Herbs

Serving: One

Ingredients:

- 2 eggs
- 1/4 cup chopped zucchini
- 1/4 cup chopped red bell pepper
- 1/4 cup chopped onion
- 1/4 cup chopped fresh herbs (parsley, basil, or dill)
- 1 tsp olive oil
- Salt and pepper

Preparation:

1. Beat the eggs in a bowl and add salt and pepper.

2. Heat the olive oil in a non-stick pan.

3. Add the zucchini, red bell pepper, and onion and sauté for 2-3 minutes.

4. Pour the eggs over the vegetables and cook until set.

5. Sprinkle the fresh herbs on top.

Approximate Nutritional Value:

Calories: 200

Protein: 10g

Fat: 10g

Carbohydrates: 10g

Fiber: 3g

Beet & Goat Cheese Dip

Serving: One

Ingredients:

• 1 medium beet

• 2 oz goat cheese

• 1/4 cup Greek yogurt

• 1 garlic clove

• 1 tbsp lemon juice

• 1 tbsp olive oil

• Salt and pepper

Preparation:

1. Preheat the oven to 400°F.

2. Wrap the beet in foil and roast for 45-60 minutes or until tender.

3. Let the beet cool, then peel and chop it.

4. Combine the chopped beet, goat cheese, Greek yogurt, minced garlic, lemon juice, olive oil, salt, and pepper in a food processor.

5. Process until smooth.

Approximate Nutritional Value:

Calories: 200

Protein: 10g

Fat: 10g

Carbohydrates: 10g

Fiber: 3g

CHAPTER THREE

Lunch Recipes

Turkey and Veggie Lettuce Wraps

Serving: One

Ingredients:
- 4 large lettuce leaves
- 4 oz cooked ground turkey
- 1/2 red bell pepper, diced
- 1/2 cucumber, diced
- 1/4 red onion, diced
- 1 tbsp olive oil
- Salt and pepper

Preparation:

1. Heat the olive oil in a pan.

2. Sauté the diced red bell pepper, cucumber, and red onion until softened.

3. Add the cooked ground turkey and season with salt and pepper.

4. Place the cooked mixture in the center of each lettuce leaf and serve.

Approximate Nutritional Value:
Calories: 200
Protein: 20g
Fat: 10g
Carbohydrates: 10g
Fiber: 3g

Caprese Salad with Balsamic Glaze

Serving: One

Ingredients:

- 4 oz fresh mozzarella, sliced
- 4 medium-sized tomatoes, sliced
- 1/4 cup fresh basil leaves
- 2 tbsp balsamic vinegar
- 1 tbsp honey

Preparation:

1. Arrange the sliced mozzarella and tomatoes on a plate.

2. Scatter the fresh basil leaves over the top.

3. In a small saucepan, combine the balsamic vinegar and honey.

4. Heat the mixture over medium heat until it thickens slightly.

5. Drizzle the balsamic glaze over the salad.

Approximate Nutritional Value:

Calories: 200

Protein: 10g

Fat: 15g

Carbohydrates: 10g

Fiber: 3g

Sweet Potato and Chickpea Buddha Bowl

Serving: One

Ingredients:
- 1 medium sweet potato, cubed
- 1/2 can chickpeas, drained and rinsed
- 1/2 red bell pepper, diced
- 1/2 cucumber, diced
- 1/4 red onion, diced
- 1 tbsp olive oil

- Salt and pepper
- 1/4 cup quinoa, cooked
- 1 tbsp tahini
- 1 tbsp lemon juice

Preparation:

1. Heat the olive oil in a pan.

2. Sauté the diced red bell pepper, cucumber, and red onion until softened.

3. Add the cubed sweet potato and chickpeas, and season with salt and pepper.

4. Cook until the sweet potato is tender.

5. In a small bowl, mix the tahini and lemon juice to make a dressing.

6. Serve the sweet potato and chickpea mixture with the cooked quinoa and tahini dressing.

Approximate Nutritional Value:
Calories: 400
Protein: 20g
Fat: 15g
Carbohydrates: 40g
Fiber: 10g

Lentil and Spinach Stuffed Peppers

Serving: One

Ingredients:
• 4 bell peppers
• 1/2 cup lentils, cooked
• 1/2 cup spinach, chopped
• 1/4 red onion, diced

- 1/4 red bell pepper, diced
- 1/4 cucumber, diced
- 1 tbsp olive oil
- Salt and pepper

Preparation:

1. Preheat the oven to 375°F.

2. Cut the bell peppers in half and remove the seeds.

3. Heat the olive oil in a pan.

4. Sauté the diced red onion, red bell pepper, and cucumber until softened.

5. Add the cooked lentils and spinach, and season with salt and pepper.

6. Stuff the bell pepper halves with the lentil and spinach mixture.

7. Bake for 20-25 minutes.

Approximate Nutritional Value:
Calories: 200
Protein: 10g
Fat: 5g
Carbohydrates: 30g
Fiber: 10g

Smoked Salmon and Leek Frittata

Ingredients:
•6 eggs
•1/2 cup smoked salmon, chopped
•1/2 leek, sliced

•1 tbsp olive oil

•Salt and pepper

Preparation:

1. Preheat the oven to 375°F.

2. Heat the olive oil in a non-stick pan.

3. Sauté the sliced leek until softened.

4. Beat the eggs in a bowl and season with salt and pepper.

5. Add the chopped smoked salmon to the pan with the leek.

6. Pour the beaten eggs over the salmon and leek mixture

7. Bake for 15-20 minutes or until the frittata is set.

Approximate Nutritional Value:

Calories: 300

Protein: 20g

Fat: 20g

Carbohydrates: 5g

Fiber: 1g

Mediterranean Pasta Salad with Shrimp and Vegetables

Serving: One

Ingredients:

•8 oz pasta, cooked

•1/2 lb shrimp, cooked and peeled

•1/2 red bell pepper, diced

•1/2 cucumber, diced

•1/4 red onion, diced

•1/4 cup cherry tomatoes, halved

- 1/4 cup feta cheese, crumbled
- 1/4 cup Kalamata olives, pitted
- 1/4 cup fresh basil leaves
- 1/4 cup olive oil
- 2 tbsp lemon juice
- Salt and pepper

Preparation:

1. Cook the pasta according to the package instructions.

2. In a large bowl, combine the cooked pasta, shrimp, diced red bell pepper, cucumber, red onion, cherry tomatoes, feta cheese, Kalamata olives, and fresh basil leaves.

3. In a small bowl, mix the olive oil, lemon juice, salt, and pepper to make a dressing.

4. Drizzle the dressing over the pasta salad.

Approximate Nutritional Value:
Calories: 400
Protein: 20g
Fat: 20g
Carbohydrates: 40g
Fiber: 5g

Stuffed Peppers with Quinoa and Ground Turkey

Serving: One

Ingredients:
• 4 bell peppers
• 1/2 cup quinoa, cooked
• 1/2 lb ground turkey
• 1/2 red bell pepper, diced

- 1/2 cucumber, diced
- 1/4 red onion, diced
- 1 tbsp olive oil
- Salt and pepper

Preparation:

1. Preheat the oven to 375°F.

2. Cut the bell peppers in half and remove the seeds.

3. Heat the olive oil in a pan.

4. Sauté the diced red bell pepper, cucumber, and red onion until softened.

Approximate Nutritional Value:
Calories: 300
Protein: 20g
Fat: 10g
Carbohydrates: 30g

Fiber: 10g

Mediterranean Chickpea Salad Sandwich

Serving: One

Ingredients:
- 1 can (15 oz) chickpeas, drained and rinsed
- 1/2 cup red bell pepper, chopped
- 1/4 cup green onions, chopped
- 3 tbsp tahini
- 2 tbsp lemon juice
- 1 tbsp olive oil
- Salt and pepper
- 2 slices of whole-grain bread
- 1/2 cup mixed greens

Preparations:

1. In a bowl, mash the chickpeas with a fork or potato masher.

2. Add the chopped red bell pepper and green onions to the bowl.

3. In a separate bowl, whisk together the tahini, lemon juice, olive oil, salt, and pepper.

4. Pour the tahini mixture over the chickpea mixture and stir to combine.

5. Toast the bread slices. Place the mixed greens on one slice of bread.

6. Spoon the chickpea salad on top of the greens.

7. Top with the other slice of bread. Serve and enjoy!

Approximate Nutritional Value:
Calories: 400

Protein: 15g

Fat: 20g

Carbohydrates: 40g

Fiber: 10

CHAPTER FOUR

Dinner Recipes

Eggplant and Chickpea Ratatouille

Serving: One

Ingredients:
- 1 eggplant, cubed
- 1 can (15 oz) chickpeas, drained and rinsed
- 1 onion, chopped
- 2 bell peppers, chopped
- 3 garlic cloves, minced
- 1 can (15 oz) diced tomatoes
- 2 tbsp olive oil
- 1 tsp dried thyme
- Salt and pepper

Preparation:

1. In a large pot, heat the olive oil over medium heat.

2. Add the chopped onion, bell peppers, and garlic. Sauté until softened.

3. Stir in the eggplant, chickpeas, diced tomatoes, and dried thyme.

4. Season with salt and pepper. Cover and simmer for 20-25 minutes.

Approximate Nutritional Value:

Calories: 350

Protein: 12g

Fat: 10g

Carbohydrates: 55g

Fiber: 15g

Lemon Herb Grilled Chicken

Serving: One

Ingredients:
- 1 boneless, skinless chicken breast
- 1 tbsp fresh lemon juice
- 1 tbsp olive oil
- 1 garlic clove, minced
- 1 tsp chopped fresh rosemary
- Salt and pepper

Preparation:

1. In a small bowl, whisk together the lemon juice, olive oil, garlic, and rosemary.

2. Season the chicken breast with salt and pepper, then brush with the lemon-herb mixture.

3. Grill the chicken over medium-high heat for 6-7 minutes per side, or until cooked through.

Approximate Nutritional Value:
Calories: 250
Protein: 30g
Fat: 10g
Carbohydrates: 2g
Fiber: 0g

Mediterranean Shrimp and Orzo Salad

Serving: One

Ingredients:
•4 oz orzo, cooked
•6 oz cooked shrimp
•1/2 cup cherry tomatoes, halved
•1/4 cup chopped cucumber

•2 tbsp chopped fresh parsley

•1 tbsp olive oil

•1 tbsp lemon juice

•Salt and pepper

Preparation:

1. In a large bowl, combine the cooked orzo, shrimp, cherry tomatoes, cucumber, and parsley.

2. Drizzle with olive oil and lemon juice.

3. Season with salt and pepper, and toss to combine.

Approximate Nutritional Value:

Calories: 300

Protein: 25g

Fat: 8g

Carbohydrates: 30g

Fiber: 3g

Lamb Kebabs with Tzatziki Sauce

Serving: One

Ingredients:
- 8 oz lamb, cubed
- 1/2 red onion, cut into chunks
- 1/2 red bell pepper, cut into chunks
- 1/4 cup plain Greek yogurt
- 1/4 cup grated cucumber
- 1 garlic clove, minced
- 1 tbsp chopped fresh dill
- 1 tbsp lemon juice
- Salt and pepper

Preparation:

1. Preheat the grill to medium-high heat.

2. Thread the lamb, red onion, and red bell pepper onto skewers. Season with salt and pepper.

3. Grill the kebabs for 10-12 minutes, turning occasionally, until the lamb is cooked to your liking.

4. In a small bowl, combine the Greek yogurt, grated cucumber, garlic, dill, and lemon juice.

5. Season with salt and pepper.

Approximate Nutritional Value:

Calories: 350

Protein: 30g

Fat: 20g

Carbohydrates: 10g

Fiber: 2g

Baked Cod with Lemon and Herbs

Serving: One

Ingredients:
- 6 oz cod fillet
- 1 tbsp olive oil
- 1 tbsp fresh lemon juice
- 1 garlic clove, minced
- 1 tsp chopped fresh parsley
- Salt and pepper

Preparation:

1. Preheat the oven to 400°F.

2. Place the cod fillet on a baking sheet lined with parchment paper.

3. In a small bowl, whisk together the olive oil, lemon juice, garlic, and parsley. Season with salt and pepper.

4. Brush the cod with the lemon-herb mixture.

5. Bake for 12-15 minutes, or until the cod is opaque and flakes easily with a fork.

Approximate Nutritional Value:

Calories: 200

Protein: 25g

Fat: 10g

Carbohydrates: 2g

Fiber: 0g

Lentil Soup with Whole-Wheat Bread

Serving: One

Ingredients:

- 1/2 cup dried lentils
- 1 carrot, chopped
- 1 celery stalk, chopped
- 1/2 onion, chopped
- 2 garlic cloves, minced
- 4 cups low-sodium vegetable broth
- 1/2 tsp ground cumin
- 1/2 tsp ground coriander
- 1/4 tsp smoked paprika
- 2 slices of whole-wheat bread

Preparation:

1. In a large pot, combine the dried lentils, carrot, celery, onion, garlic, vegetable broth, cumin, coriander, and smoked paprika.

2. Bring to a boil, then reduce the heat and simmer for 25-30 minutes, or until the lentils are tender.

3. Season with salt and pepper. Serve the lentil soup with whole-wheat bread.

Approximate Nutritional Value:
Calories: 300
Protein: 20g
Fat: 5g
Carbohydrates: 50g
Fiber: 15g

Greek Shrimp Scampi with Whole-Wheat Pasta

Serving: One

Ingredients:
- 4 oz whole-wheat spaghetti, cooked
- 6 oz large shrimp, peeled and deveined
- 2 garlic cloves, minced
- 1/4 cup chopped fresh parsley
- 1/4 cup crumbled feta cheese

•2 tbsp olive oil

•2 tbsp fresh lemon juice

•Salt and pepper

Preparation:

1. In a large skillet, heat the olive oil over medium heat.

2. Add the minced garlic and cook for 1 minute.

3. Add the shrimp and cook for 2-3 minutes per side, or until pink and opaque.

4. Stir in the cooked whole-wheat spaghetti, fresh lemon juice, and chopped fresh parsley. Season with salt and pepper.

5. Sprinkle with crumbled feta cheese before serving.

Approximate Nutritional Value:

Calories: 400

Protein: 30g

Fat: 15g

Carbohydrates: 35g

Fiber: 6g

Mediterranean Stuffed Bell Peppers

Serving: One

Ingredients:
- 2 bell peppers
- 1/2 cup cooked quinoa
- 1/2 cup canned chickpeas, drained and rinsed
- 1/4 cup chopped cucumber
- 1/4 cup chopped fresh parsley
- 2 tbsp crumbled feta cheese
- 1 tbsp olive oil
- 1 tbsp lemon juice
- Salt and pepper

Preparation:

1. Preheat the oven to 375°F.

2. Cut the bell peppers in half and remove the seeds.

3. In a large bowl, combine the cooked quinoa, chickpeas, chopped cucumber, chopped fresh parsley, crumbled feta cheese, olive oil, and lemon juice. Season with salt and pepper.

4. Stuff the bell pepper halves with the quinoa and chickpea mixture.

5. Bake for 20-25 minutes, or until the bell peppers are tender.

Approximate Nutritional Value:

Calories: 350

Protein: 15g

Fat: 10g
Carbohydrates: 45g
Fiber: 10g

Parmesan Eggplant

Serving: One

Ingredients:
- 1 small eggplant, sliced
- 1/4 cup grated Parmesan cheese
- 1/4 cup whole-wheat breadcrumbs
- 1 egg, beaten
- 1/2 cup marinara sauce
- 1/4 cup shredded mozzarella cheese
- 1 tbsp olive oil
- Salt and pepper

Preparation:

1. Preheat the oven to 400°F.

2. In one shallow dish, combine the Parmesan cheese and whole-wheat breadcrumbs.

3. In another shallow dish, place the beaten egg.

4. Dip the eggplant slices in the beaten egg, then dredge in the Parmesan-breadcrumb mixture, pressing to adhere.

5. Place the coated eggplant slices on a baking sheet lined with parchment paper.

6. Drizzle with olive oil and season with salt and pepper.

7. Bake for 15-20 minutes, or until the eggplant is golden and tender.

8. Remove from the oven and top each eggplant slice with marinara sauce and shredded mozzarella cheese.

9. Return to the oven and bake for an additional 5 minutes, or until the cheese is melted and bubbly.

Approximate Nutritional Value:

Calories: 300

Protein: 15g

Fat: 15g

Carbohydrates: 25g

Fiber: 8g

CHAPTER FIVE

Snacks And Appetizers

Cheesy Kale Chips

Serving: One

Ingredients:
- 2 cups kale, stems removed and torn into pieces
- 1 tbsp olive oil
- 2 tbsp nutritional yeast
- Salt to taste

Preparation:

1. Preheat the oven to 275°F.

2. In a large bowl, massage the kale with olive oil and salt.

3. Sprinkle with nutritional yeast and toss to coat.

4. Spread the kale in a single layer on a baking sheet.

5. Bake for 20-25 minutes, or until crisp.

Approximate Nutritional Value:

Calories: 100

Protein: 5g

Fat: 7g

Carbohydrates: 10g

Fiber: 3g

Greek Yogurt Dip with Cucumber and Mint

Serving: One

Ingredients:

• 1/2 cup Greek yogurt

- 1/4 cup cucumber, finely chopped
- 1 tbsp fresh mint, chopped
- 1/2 tsp lemon juice
- Salt and pepper to taste

Preparation:

1. In a small bowl, combine the Greek yogurt, cucumber, mint, and lemon juice.

2. Season with salt and pepper.

Approximate Nutritional Value:

Calories: 50

Protein: 7g

Fat: 1g

Carbohydrates: 3g

Fiber: 1g

Roasted Chickpeas with Spices

Serving: One

Ingredients:
- 1 can (15 oz) chickpeas, drained, rinsed, and patted dry
- 1 tbsp olive oil
- 1 tsp ground cumin
- 1/2 tsp smoked paprika
- 1/2 tsp garlic powder
- Salt to taste

Preparation:

1. Preheat the oven to 400°F.

2. In a bowl, toss the chickpeas with olive oil, cumin, paprika, garlic powder, and salt.

3. Spread the chickpeas on a baking sheet in a single layer.

4. Roast for 20-30 minutes, or until crispy.

Approximate Nutritional Value:
Calories: 150
Protein: 6g
Fat: 4g
Carbohydrates: 20g
Fiber: 5g

Stuffed Dates with Nuts and Goat Cheese

Serving: One

Ingredients:
- 3 Medjool dates, pitted
- 1 tbsp goat cheese
- 3 almonds, walnuts, or pecans

Preparation:
1. Gently open the dates and remove the pits.

2. Stuff each date with 1 teaspoon of goat cheese and 1 nut.

Approximate Nutritional Value:
Calories: 100
Protein: 3g
Fat: 4g
Carbohydrates: 15g
Fiber: 2g

Edamame Pods

Serving: One

Ingredients:
•1 cup edamame pods
•Salt to taste

Preparation:

1. Boil the edamame pods in salted water for 3-5 minutes.

2. Drain and pat dry before serving.

Approximate Nutritional Value:
Calories: 100
Protein: 9g
Fat: 3g
Carbohydrates: 8g
Fiber: 4g

Greek Salad with Feta Cheese

Serving: One

Ingredients:
- 1 cup mixed greens
- 1/4 cup cucumber, sliced
- 1/4 cup cherry tomatoes, halved
- 2 tbsp Kalamata olives
- 1/4 cup feta cheese, crumbled
- 1 tbsp extra virgin olive oil
- 1/2 tbsp red wine vinegar
- Salt and pepper to taste

Preparation:

1. In a large bowl, combine the mixed greens, cucumber, tomatoes, and olives.

2. Drizzle with olive oil and red wine vinegar.

3. Season with salt and pepper. Top with crumbled feta cheese.

Approximate Nutritional Value:

Calories: 150

Protein: 5g

Fat: 10g

Carbohydrates: 10g

Fiber: 3g

Hummus and Roasted Veggies

Serving: One

Ingredients:

•1/4 cup hummus

•1 cup mixed roasted vegetables (bell peppers, zucchini, eggplant, etc.)

Preparation:

1. Serve the hummus with the mixed roasted vegetables for dipping.

Approximate Nutritional Value:

Calories: 150

Protein: 5g

Fat: 7g

Carbohydrates: 20g

Fiber: 6g

Power Balls

Serving: One

Ingredients:
- 1/2 cup rolled oats
- 1/4 cup nut butter
- 2 tbsp honey
- 2 tbsp chia seeds
- 2 tbsp dark chocolate chips
- 1/4 tsp vanilla extract

Preparation:

1. In a bowl, mix all the ingredients.

2. Roll the mixture into small balls and refrigerate until firm.

Approximate Nutritional Value:
Calories: 200
Protein: 6g
Fat: 10g
Carbohydrates: 20g
Fiber: 5g

Greek Spinach and Feta Dip

Serving: One

Ingredients:
- 1/2 cup Greek yogurt
- 1/4 cup feta cheese, crumbled
- 1/2 cup cooked spinach, chopped
- 1/4 tsp garlic powder
- Salt and pepper to taste

Preparation:

1. In a bowl, mix all the ingredients.

2. Serve with whole-grain pita chips or vegetable sticks for dipping.

Approximate Nutritional Value:
Calories: 150
Protein: 10g
Fat: 8g

Carbohydrates: 10g

Fiber: 3g

Tomato and Basil Bruschetta

Serving: One

Ingredients:

- •2 slices whole-grain baguette
- •1/2 cup cherry tomatoes, diced
- •1/4 cup fresh basil, chopped
- •1/2 tbsp balsamic vinegar
- •1/2 tbsp extra virgin olive oil
- •1 garlic clove, minced
- •Salt and pepper to taste

Preparation:

1. In a bowl, mix the cherry tomatoes, basil, balsamic vinegar, olive oil, and garlic.

2. Season with salt and pepper.

3. Toast the whole-grain baguette slices and top with the tomato mixture.

Approximate Nutritional Value:

Calories: 150

Protein: 5g

Fat: 5g

Carbohydrates: 20g

Fiber: 3g

CHAPTER SIX

Fish And Seafood

Mediterranean Grilled Salmon

Serving: One

Ingredients:
- 4 oz salmon fillet
- 1 tbsp extra virgin olive oil
- 1/2 tsp dried oregano
- 1/2 tsp dried basil
- Salt and pepper to taste

Preparation:

1. Preheat the grill to medium-high heat.

2. In a small bowl, mix the olive oil, oregano, basil, salt, and pepper.

3. Brush the salmon fillet with the olive oil mixture.

4. Grill the salmon for 4-5 minutes per side, or until cooked through.

Approximate Nutritional Value:
Calories: 200
Protein: 20g
Fat: 12g
Carbohydrates: 0g
Fiber: 0g

Lemon Garlic Shrimp Skewers

Serving: One

Ingredients:
•4 oz shrimp, peeled and deveined
•1 tbsp extra virgin olive oil
•1 garlic clove, minced
•1/2 lemon, juiced

•Salt and pepper to taste

Preparation:

1. Preheat the grill to medium-high heat.

1. In a small bowl, mix the olive oil, garlic, lemon juice, salt, and pepper.

3. Thread the shrimp onto skewers.

4. Brush the shrimp with the olive oil mixture.

5. Grill the shrimp for 2-3 minutes per side, or until cooked through.

Approximate Nutritional Value:
Calories: 100
Protein: 15g
Fat: 4g
Carbohydrates: 2g   Fiber: 0g

Herb-Crusted Tuna Steaks

Serving: One

Ingredients:
- 4 oz tuna steak
- 1 tbsp extra virgin olive oil
- 1/4 cup whole wheat breadcrumbs
- 1 tbsp fresh parsley, chopped
- 1 tbsp fresh thyme, chopped
- Salt and pepper to taste

Preparation:

1. Preheat the oven to 400°F.

2. In a small bowl, mix the breadcrumbs, parsley, thyme, salt, and pepper.

3. Brush the tuna steak with the olive oil.

4. Press the breadcrumb mixture onto both sides of the tuna steak.

5. Place the tuna steak on a baking sheet.

6. Bake for 10-12 minutes, or until cooked through.

Approximate Nutritional Value:
Calories: 200
Protein: 25g
Fat: 7g
Carbohydrates: 8g
Fiber: 2g

Greek Style Baked Tilapia

Serving: One

Ingredients:
- 4 oz tilapia fillet
- 1/4 cup cherry tomatoes, halved

- 1/4 cup Kalamata olives, pitted and chopped
- 1/4 cup feta cheese, crumbled
- 1 tbsp extra virgin olive oil
- 1/2 tbsp lemon juice
- Salt and pepper to taste

Preparation:

1. Preheat the oven to 375°F.

2. In a small bowl, mix the olive oil, lemon juice, salt, and pepper.

3. Place the tilapia fillet on a baking sheet.

4. Top the tilapia with the cherry tomatoes, Kalamata olives, and feta cheese.

5. Drizzle the olive oil mixture over the top.

6. Bake for 15-20 minutes, or until cooked through.

Approximate Nutritional Value:

Calories: 200

Protein: 20g

Fat: 10g

Carbohydrates: 5g

Fiber: 1g

Lemon Herb Marinated Swordfish

Serving: One

Ingredients:
- •4 oz swordfish steak
- •1 tbsp extra virgin olive oil
- •1/2 lemon, juiced
- •1 garlic clove, minced
- •1 tbsp fresh parsley, chopped
- •1 tbsp fresh thyme, chopped
- •Salt and pepper to taste

Preparation:

1. In a small bowl, mix the olive oil, lemon juice, garlic, parsley, thyme, salt, and pepper.

2. Place the swordfish steak in a shallow dish.

3. Pour the marinade over the swordfish.

4. Cover and refrigerate for at least 30 minutes.

5. Preheat the grill to medium-high heat.

6. Grill the swordfish for 4-5 minutes per side, or until cooked through.

Approximate Nutritional Value:
Calories: 200

Protein: 25g

Fat: 9g

Carbohydrates: 2g

Fiber: 0g

Mediterranean Scallop Salad

Serving: One

Ingredients:
- 4 oz scallops
- 2 cups mixed greens
- 1/4 cup cherry tomatoes, halved
- 1/4 cup cucumber, sliced
- 1/4 cup Kalamata olives, pitted
- 1/4 cup feta cheese, crumbled
- 1 tbsp extra virgin olive oil
- 1/2 tbsp red wine vinegar
- Salt and pepper to taste

Preparation:

1. In a small bowl, mix the olive oil, red wine vinegar, salt, and pepper.

2. Heat a non-stick skillet over medium-high heat.

3. Add the scallops and cook for 2-3 minutes per side, or until cooked through.

4. In a large bowl, combine the mixed greens, cherry tomatoes, cucumber, Kalamata olives, and feta cheese.

5. Drizzle the olive oil mixture over the top. Top with the cooked scallops.

Approximate Nutritional Value:

Calories: 200

Protein: 20g

Fat: 12g

Carbohydrates: 8g

Fiber: 3g

Baked Salmon with Lemon and Dill

Serving: One

Ingredients:
- 4 oz salmon fillet
- 1 tbsp extra virgin olive oil
- 1/2 lemon, sliced
- 1 tbsp fresh dill, chopped
- Salt and pepper to taste

Preparation:

1. Preheat the oven to 375°F.

2. Brush the salmon fillet with the olive oil. Season with salt and pepper.

3. Top the salmon with the lemon slices and fresh dill.

4. Bake for 15-20 minutes, or until cooked through.

Approximate Nutritional Value:
Calories: 250
Protein: 25g
Fat: 15g
Carbohydrates: 2g
Fiber: 1g

Anchovy and Olive Tapenade

Serving: One

Ingredients:
- 1/2 cup pitted Kalamata olives
- 1/4 cup anchovy fillets
- 2 tbsp capers
- 1 garlic clove
- 2 tbsp fresh parsley
- 2 tbsp extra virgin olive oil
- 1/2 lemon, juiced

Preparation:

1. In a food processor, combine the olives, anchovies, capers, garlic, and parsley.

2. Pulse until the mixture is finely chopped.

3. Transfer the mixture to a bowl and stir in the olive oil and lemon juice.

Approximate Nutritional Value:
Calories: 150
Protein: 5g
Fat: 12g
Carbohydrates: 4g
Fiber: 2g

Grilled   Halibut   with
Mediterranean Salsa

Serving: One

Ingredients:
- 4 oz halibut fillet
- 1 tbsp extra virgin olive oil
- 1/2 tsp dried oregano
- 1/2 tsp dried basil
- Salt and pepper to taste

Mediterranean Salsa:
- 1/2 cup cherry tomatoes, diced
- 1/4 cup cucumber, diced
- 2 tbsp red onion, finely chopped
- 1 tbsp fresh parsley, chopped
- 1 tbsp red wine vinegar
- 1 tbsp extra virgin olive oil
- Salt and pepper to taste

Preparation:

1. Preheat the grill to medium-high heat.

2. Brush the halibut fillet with the olive oil.

3. Season with oregano, basil, salt, and pepper.

4. Grill the halibut for 3-4 minutes per side, or until cooked through.

5. In a bowl, combine the cherry tomatoes, cucumber, red onion, parsley, red wine vinegar, and olive oil to make the salsa.

6. Serve the grilled halibut with the Mediterranean salsa on top.

Approximate Nutritional Value:
Calories: 200
Protein: 25g

Fat: 10g

Carbohydrates: 5g

Fiber: 2g

CHAPTER SEVEN

Dessert Recipes

Coconut Chia Pudding with Berries

Serving: One

Ingredients:
- 1/2 cup unsweetened coconut milk
- 2 tbsp chia seeds
- 1/4 tsp vanilla extract
- 1/2 cup mixed berries

Preparation:

1. In a small bowl, whisk together the coconut milk, chia seeds, and vanilla extract.

2. Cover and refrigerate for at least 2 hours, or overnight.

3. Top with mixed berries before serving.

Approximate Nutritional Value:
Calories: 150
Protein: 4g
Fat: 10g
Carbohydrates: 12g
Fiber: 7g

Yogurt and Honey Panna Cotta

Serving: One

Ingredients:
- 1/2 cup plain Greek yogurt
- 1/2 cup unsweetened almond milk
- 1 tbsp honey
- 1 tsp vanilla extract
- 1/2 tsp gelatin powder

Preparation:

1. In a small saucepan, heat the almond milk over medium heat.

2. Whisk in the honey, vanilla extract, and gelatin powder until dissolved.

3. Remove from heat and whisk in the Greek yogurt.

4. Pour the mixture into a ramekin or small bowl.

5. Cover and refrigerate for at least 2 hours, or until set.

Approximate Nutritional Value:

Calories: 150

Protein: 12g

Fat: 6g

Carbohydrates: 12g   Fiber: 1g

Fig and Walnut Energy Bites

Serving: One

Ingredients:
- 1/2 cup dried figs
- 1/2 cup walnuts
- 1/4 cup almond flour
- 1/4 tsp cinnamon
- Pinch of salt

Preparation:
1. In a food processor, pulse the dried figs and walnuts until finely chopped.

2. Add the almond flour, cinnamon, and salt. Pulse until well combined.

3. Roll the mixture into small balls.

4. Store in an airtight container in the refrigerator.

Approximate Nutritional Value:

Calories: 150

Protein: 4g

Fat: 10g

Carbohydrates: 14g

Fiber: 3g

Pistachio and Dark Chocolate Bark

Serving: One

Ingredients:
- 1/4 cup shelled pistachios
- 1/4 cup dark chocolate chips

Preparation:

1. Line a baking sheet with parchment paper.

Melt the dark chocolate chips in a double boiler or the microwave.

2. Pour the melted chocolate onto the prepared baking sheet.

3. Sprinkle the pistachios over the top.

4. Refrigerate for at least 30 minutes, or until set.

5. Break into pieces before serving.

Approximate Nutritional Value:

Calories: 150

Protein: 3g

Fat: 10g

Carbohydrates: 14g

Fiber: 3g

Almond Flour Banana Bread

Serving: One

Ingredients:

- 1 ripe banana, mashed
- 1 egg
- 1/2 cup almond flour
- 1/4 cup unsweetened applesauce
- 1/2 tsp baking powder
- 1/2 tsp cinnamon
- Pinch of salt

Preparation:

1. Preheat the oven to 350°F.

2. In a large bowl, whisk together the mashed banana and egg.

3. Add the almond flour, applesauce, baking powder, cinnamon, and salt. Stir until well combined.

4. Pour the mixture into a greased loaf pan.

5. Bake for 25-30 minutes, or until a toothpick inserted into the center comes out clean.

Approximate Nutritional Value:
Calories: 200
Protein: 7g
Fat: 12g
Carbohydrates: 18g
Fiber: 4g

Mediterranean Fruit Salad with Mint

Serving: One

Ingredients:
• 1 cup mixed fruit (such as berries, grapes, and melon)
• 1 tbsp fresh mint, chopped
• 1 tsp honey

• 1 tsp lemon juice

Preparation:

1. In a small bowl, whisk together the mint, honey, and lemon juice.
2. Pour the mixture over the mixed fruit.

3. Toss to coat.

Approximate Nutritional Value:
Calories: 100
Protein: 1g
Fat: 0g
Carbohydrates: 25g
Fiber: 3g

Pumpkin Spice Muffins

Serving: One

Ingredients:

- 1/2 cup almond flour
- 1/4 cup coconut flour
- 1/4 cup pumpkin puree
- 2 eggs
- 1/4 cup honey
- 1 tsp baking powder
- 1 tsp pumpkin pie spice
- Pinch of salt

Preparation:

1. Preheat the oven to 350°F.

2. In a large bowl, whisk together the almond flour, coconut flour, baking powder, pumpkin pie spice, and salt.

3. In a separate bowl, whisk together the pumpkin puree, eggs, and honey.

4. Add the wet ingredients to the dry ingredients and stir until well combined.

5. Pour the mixture into a greased muffin tin.

6. Bake for 20-25 minutes, or until a toothpick inserted into the center comes out clean.

Approximate Nutritional Value:

Calories: 150

Protein: 5g

Fat: 8g

Carbohydrates: 16g

Fiber: 4g

Coconut Macaroons

Serving: One

Ingredients:

- 1/2 cup unsweetened shredded coconut
- 1 egg white

•1 tbsp honey
•1/4 tsp vanilla extract
•Pinch of salt

Preparation:

1. Preheat the oven to 350°F.

2. In a small bowl, whisk together the egg white, honey, vanilla extract, and salt.

3. Stir in the shredded coconut.

4. Drop the mixture by spoonfuls onto a baking sheet lined with parchment paper.

5. Bake for 10-12 minutes, or until golden brown.

Approximate Nutritional Value:
Calories: 100
Protein: 2g

Fat: 7g

Carbohydrates: 8g

Mixed Berry Sorbet

Serving: One

Ingredients:
- 3 cups frozen mixed berries
- 3 tbsp honey
- 1/4-1/2 cup warm water

Preparation:

1. Add frozen fruit and honey into a food processor. Pulse lightly to mix up frozen fruit.

2. Add warm water, starting with 1/4 cup and adding more as needed, until the mixture is smooth and creamy.

3. Pour the mixture into a freezer-safe container and freeze for at least 30 minutes before serving.

4. Your freezing time will depend on what consistency you want the sorbet to be. If you want a softer consistency, freeze it just for 30 minutes or so. For a firmer consistency, freeze it longer.

Approximate Nutritional Value:

Calories: 100

Protein: 1g

Fat: 0g

Carbohydrates: 26g

Fiber: 4g

CHAPTER EIGHT

Lifestyle Tips For IVF Success

Stress Management Strategies

Stress management is a crucial component of navigating the In Vitro Fertilization (IVF) journey. Implementing effective strategies to mitigate stress can positively impact both physical and emotional well-being, ultimately enhancing the chances of IVF success. Firstly, prioritize self-care practices such as mindfulness meditation, deep breathing exercises, and yoga to promote relaxation and reduce tension. Engage in regular physical activity, such as walking, swimming, or gentle stretching, to release endorphins and alleviate stress.

Additionally, maintain open communication with your partner, family, and friends, sharing your feelings and seeking support when needed. Establish healthy boundaries and prioritize activities that bring joy and fulfillment. Consider incorporating holistic therapies such as acupuncture, massage therapy, or aromatherapy to further enhance relaxation and reduce stress levels. Finally, practice gratitude and positive thinking, focusing on the present moment and maintaining optimism about the IVF process. By incorporating these stress management strategies into your lifestyle, you can cultivate a supportive environment conducive to IVF success, fostering emotional resilience and overall well-being throughout the journey.

Physical Activity and Exercise Guidelines

Physical activity and exercise play a vital role in promoting overall health and optimizing the chances of success during the In Vitro Fertilization (IVF) process. Engaging in regular exercise not only helps to maintain a healthy weight but also reduces stress, improves circulation, and enhances mood, all of which can positively impact fertility outcomes.

For individuals undergoing IVF, it's important to follow exercise guidelines that balance physical activity with rest and recovery. Aim for moderate-intensity exercise most days of the week, incorporating a variety of activities to promote cardiovascular health, strength, and flexibility.

Here are five best exercises perfect for people undergoing IVF:

Walking: Simply lace up your shoes and head outdoors or hop on a treadmill. Start with a brisk walk for 30 minutes, gradually increasing duration and intensity as tolerated.

Yoga: Practice gentle yoga poses that focus on relaxation, stress reduction, and pelvic floor strengthening. Incorporate poses such as Child's Pose, Cat-Cow, and Pigeon Pose into your routine.

Swimming: Take a dip in the pool for a low-impact, full-body workout. Swim laps or participate in water aerobics classes to improve cardiovascular fitness and muscle tone.

Cycling: Whether on a stationary bike or outdoors, cycling provides an effective cardiovascular workout while being gentle on the joints.

Start with a moderate pace for 20-30 minutes, gradually increasing duration and intensity.

Strength Training: Incorporate resistance exercises using body weight, dumbbells, or resistance bands to build muscle strength and endurance. Focus on exercises such as squats, lunges, push-ups, and planks, performing 8-12 repetitions of each exercise.

Remember to listen to your body and consult with your healthcare provider before starting any new exercise program, especially during fertility treatments. By incorporating regular physical activity and following these exercise guidelines, you can optimize your overall health and improve your chances of IVF success.

Hydration and Its Impact on Fertility

Hydration plays a critical role in fertility and can significantly impact the success of the In Vitro Fertilization (IVF) process. Proper hydration is essential for maintaining optimal reproductive function, supporting egg and sperm health, and creating an optimal environment for embryo implantation.

Adequate hydration ensures that the body's systems, including the reproductive organs, function optimally. It helps regulate hormone levels, improve blood flow to the reproductive organs, and facilitate the production of cervical mucus, which is crucial for sperm motility and transport.

Furthermore, staying well-hydrated can help prevent conditions such as urinary tract infections (UTIs) and constipation, which can negatively affect fertility and overall comfort during the IVF process. For individuals undergoing IVF, it's important to prioritize hydration by drinking plenty of water throughout the day. Aim to consume at least 8-10 glasses of water daily, and adjust your intake based on activity level, climate, and individual needs.

In addition to water, incorporating hydrating foods such as fruits, vegetables, and herbal teas can also contribute to overall hydration levels. By maintaining optimal hydration, individuals undergoing IVF can support their reproductive health and improve their chances of success. Making hydration a priority is a simple yet effective lifestyle strategy that can positively impact fertility outcomes during the IVF journey.

14-DAY MEAL PLAN

Day 1

Breakfast: Greek Yogurt Bowl with Berries and Nuts
Lunch: Turkey and Veggie Lettuce Wraps
Dinner: Eggplant and Chickpea Ratatouille

Day 2

Breakfast: Mediterranean Flatbread Pizza
Lunch: Caprese Salad with Balsamic Glaze
Dinner: Lemon Herb Grilled Chicken

Day 3

Breakfast: Turkish Menemen
Lunch: Sweet Potato and Chickpea Buddha Bowl
Dinner: Mediterranean Shrimp and Orzo Salad

Day 4

Breakfast: Avocado and Tomato Toast

Lunch: Lentil and Spinach Stuffed Peppers

Dinner: Lamb Kebabs with Tzatziki Sauce

Day 5

Breakfast: Mediterranean Veggie Omelette

Lunch: Smoked salmon and leek frittata

Dinner: Baked Cod with Lemon and Herbs

Day 6

Breakfast: Mediterranean Shakshuka

Lunch: Mediterranean Pasta Salad with Shrimp and Vegetables

Dinner: Lentil Soup with Whole-Wheat Bread

Day 7

Breakfast: Smoked Salmon and Cream Cheese Bagel

Lunch: Stuffed Peppers with Quinoa and Ground Turkey

Dinner: Greek Shrimp Scampi with Whole-Wheat Pasta

Day 8

Breakfast: Frittata with Vegetables and Herbs

Lunch: Mediterranean Chickpea Salad Sandwich

Dinner: Mediterranean Stuffed Bell Peppers

Day 9

Breakfast: Beet & Goat Cheese Dip

Lunch: Turkey and Veggie Lettuce Wraps

Dinner: Parmesan Eggplant

Day 10

Breakfast: Greek Yogurt Bowl with Berries and Nuts

Lunch: Caprese Salad with Balsamic Glaze

Dinner: Lemon Herb Grilled Chicken

Day 11

Breakfast: Mediterranean Flatbread Pizza
Lunch: Sweet Potato and Chickpea Buddha Bowl
Dinner: Mediterranean Shrimp and Orzo Salad

Day 12

Breakfast: Avocado and Tomato Toast
Lunch: Lentil and Spinach Stuffed Peppers
Dinner: Lamb Kebabs with Tzatziki Sauce

Day 13

Breakfast: Mediterranean Veggie Omelette
Lunch: Smoked salmon and leek frittata
Dinner: Baked Cod with Lemon and Herbs

Day 14

Breakfast: Mediterranean Shakshuka

Lunch: Mediterranean Pasta Salad with Shrimp and Vegetables

Dinner: Lentil Soup with Whole-Wheat Bread

CONCLUSION

In concluding this Mediterranean Diet Cookbook for IVF, we celebrate the harmonious fusion of vibrant flavors and fertility-supportive nutrients within these carefully curated recipes. The Mediterranean diet, with its emphasis on fresh produce, lean proteins, and heart-healthy fats, emerges as not just a culinary delight but a lifestyle tailored to nurture reproductive health during the In Vitro Fertilization journey.

Through breakfasts brimming with antioxidants, lunches packed with nutrient-dense ingredients, dinners featuring wholesome proteins, and delightful snacks, this cookbook provides a holistic approach to nutrition that aligns with the intricacies of fertility. From the zesty Greek Yogurt Bowl with Berries to the aromatic Lemon Herb

Grilled Chicken and the guilt-free indulgence of Coconut Chia Pudding with Berries, each recipe is crafted to fuel your body with the essential elements required for optimal reproductive well-being. As you embark on this culinary voyage, consider it not merely as a set of recipes but as a lifestyle shift, a commitment to nourishing your body and soul. The Mediterranean Diet, with its roots in a region renowned for health and longevity, beckons you to embrace not just a way of eating but a way of living. Its timeless principles transcend mere sustenance, offering a path to holistic well-being. In adopting and adapting to this diet, envision the transformation beyond the kitchen. Picture the synergy between flavorful meals and a rejuvenated body, fostering an environment conducive to the fertility journey.

Embrace this cookbook as a companion, guiding you towards a lifestyle that intertwines nutrition, joy, and the hope for a beautiful new chapter. May each culinary creation serve as a testament to your commitment to fertility, health, and the flourishing life that lies ahead. Your journey is unique, and this cookbook is your partner in making it a nourishing, flavorful, and ultimately successful one. Cheers to your health, happiness, and the possibilities that a Mediterranean-inspired lifestyle holds for you on this incredible IVF journey.

Printed in Great Britain
by Amazon

42636070R00076